MW01289842

180
"Notable Quotable Anger Management Tips"

on

Anger, Stress, Depression, Loneliness, Loss and Emotional Intelligence (EQ)

Gregory D. Anderson, Jr., C.A.M.F.
Certified Anger Management Facilitator

CONTENTS

INTRODUCTION

Though anger is an emotion fueled by discontent, we should not view anger as the solution to discontent. Anger is a response that can be and should be controlled as the misuse of this response often leads to negative outcomes. For this reason, 180 Notable Quotable Anger Management Tips on Anger, Stress, Depression, Loneliness, Loss and Emotional Intelligence (EQ) provides valuable, thought-provoking quotes to center the mind, to address emotions, and ultimately to control behaviors that stem from anger.

Each section, Anger, Stress, Depression, Loneliness, Loss and Emotional Intelligence (EQ), focuses on a specific topic and concludes with open-ended discussion questions, thus creating a space to isolate and identify emotional triggers and to develop effective responses to these triggers. Carefully read, recite and reflect on the quotes in each section then use the discussion questions to apply the information you acquire during your moments of reflection. Make 180 Notable Quotable Anger Management Tips on Anger, Stress, Depression, Loneliness, Loss and Emotional Intelligence (EQ) a daily commitment and begin to take control of your life. May this simple yet direct guide be your primary resource for effective anger management.

"Notable Quotable Anger Management Tips"

ANGER

Anger is an emotion that stems from discontentment with and hostility toward a person or thing. It is commonly associated with feelings of rage, wrath and aggression. Even though anger can indicate suppressed negative feelings and influence solutions to underlying issues, anger often serves as a threat to an individual's physical health and emotional and mental well-being.

(Source: American Psychological Association)

Holding on to anger is like grasping a hot coal with the intent of throwing it at someone else; you are the one who gets burned. ~Buddha

You will not be punished for your anger; you will be punished by your anger. ~Buddha

Every day we have plenty of opportunities to get angry, stressed or offended. But what you're doing when you indulge these negative emotions is giving something outside yourself power over your happiness. You can choose to not let little things upset you. ~Joel Osteen

"Notable Quotable Anger Management Tips"

ANGER

People won't have time for you if you are always angry or complaining. ~Stephen Hawking

In times of great stress or adversity, it's always best to keep busy, to plow your anger and your energy into something positive. ~Lee Iacocca

When anger rises, think of the consequences. ~Confucius

"Notable Quotable Anger Management Tips"

ANGER

When angry, count to ten before you speak. If very angry, count to one hundred. ~Thomas Jefferson

Anger is an acid that can do more harm to the vessel in which it is stored than to anything on which it is poured. ~Mark Twain

Discussion is an exchange of knowledge; an argument an exchange of ignorance. ~Robert Quillen

"Notable Quotable Anger Management Tips"

ANGER

Let us not look back in anger nor forward in fear, but around in awareness. ~James Thurber

Usually when people are sad, they don't do anything. They just cry over their condition. But when they get angry, they bring about a change.
~James Russell Lowell

There's nothing wrong with anger provided you use it constructively. ~Wayne Dyer

"Notable Quotable Anger Management Tips"

ANGER

Sometimes, you have to get angry to get things done. ~Ang Lee

I shall allow no man to belittle my soul by making me hate him. ~Booker T. Washington

The opposite of anger is not calmness; it's empathy. ~Mehmet Oz

"Notable Quotable Anger Management Tips"

ANGER

Anger ventilated often hurries towards forgiveness; anger concealed often hardens into revenge.
~Edward G. Bulwer-Lytton

We boil at different degrees. ~Clint Eastwood

In a controversy, the instant we feel anger we have already ceased striving for the truth and have begun striving for ourselves. ~Buddha

"Notable Quotable Anger Management Tips"

ANGER

He who angers you conquers you. ~Elizabeth Kenny

Love implies anger. The man who is angered by nothing cares about nothing. ~Edward Abbey

There is nothing that so much gratifies an ill tongue as when it finds an angry heart. ~Thomas Fuller

"Notable Quotable Anger Management Tips"

ANGER

Anger is a momentary madness, so control your passion or it will control you. ~G. M. Trevelyan

There was never an angry man that thought his anger unjust. ~Saint Francis de Sales

Anger, if not restrained, is frequently more hurtful to us than the injury that provokes it.
~Lucius Annaeus Seneca

"Notable Quotable Anger Management Tips"

ANGER

When you lose control, who are you giving the remote control? ~Gregory D. Anderson, Jr.

What you are angry about in this moment fifty years from now it really won't matter?
~Gregory D. Anderson, Jr.

Don't allow your anger to paralyze you into an extreme level of hate or rage with anyone because it can be detrimental to your health. ~Gregory D. Anderson, Jr.

"Notable Quotable Anger Management Tips"

ANGER

Let your anger drive you to be more productive, resourceful and focus without allowing that thief called procrastination to rob you of your time.
~Gregory D. Anderson, Jr.

Anger isn't always bad; in fact this emotion is normal but what makes it defective, destructive and dangerous is when one's actions become harmful to one's self or others. ~Gregory D. Anderson, Jr.

Smile despite your anger or storm that battles within you. Grab a journal or notepad and jot down those things which bother you daily in order to improve conflict resolution. ~Gregory D. Anderson, Jr.

On the next few lines, describe your definition of anger.

_____

_____

_____

_____

What events have shaped your definition of anger? What triggers your anger?

_____

_____

_____

_____

How do you typically address anger? In what ways can you now improve your response to anger?

_____

_____

_____

_____

Imagine you are face-to-face with your anger. How would you confront it? What would you do or say to overcome it?

_____

_____

_____

_____

_____

"Notable Quotable Anger Management Tips"

STRESS

Stress is emotional discomfort typically caused by changes in an individual's environment. Often accompanied by anxiety, a significant amount of stress can cause mental, emotional and physical changes that could possibly lead to serious health issues. Though some individuals perform well in stressful situations, some individuals find stress overwhelming and difficult to manage.

(Source: American Psychological Association)

The greatest weapon against stress is our ability to choose one thought over another. ~William James

All the suffering, stress, and addiction comes from not realizing you already are what you are looking for. ~Jon Kabat-Zinn

It's not stress that kills us; it is our reaction to it. ~Hans Selye

"Notable Quotable Anger Management Tips"

STRESS

You need to be able to manage stress because hard times will come, and a positive outlook is what gets you through. ~Marie Osmond

Being in control of your life and having realistic expectations about your day-to-day challenges are the keys to stress management, which is perhaps the most important ingredient to living a happy, healthy and rewarding life. ~Marilu Henner

Letting go helps us to live in a more peaceful state of mind and helps restore our balance. It allows others to be responsible for themselves and for us to take our hands off situations that do not belong to us. This frees us from unnecessary stress. ~Melody Beattie

"Notable Quotable Anger Management Tips"

STRESS

If you don't think your anxiety, depression, sadness and stress impact your physical health, think again. All of these emotions trigger chemical reactions in your body, which can lead to inflammation and a weakened immune system. Learn how to cope, sweet friend. There will always be dark days. ~Kris Carr

Stress is the negative whirlwind of emotions that gets imposed on top of our stimulation and engagement. ~Andrew J. Bernstein

I treat myself pretty good. I take lots of vacations; I eat well; I take supplements; I do mercury detox; I get plenty of sleep; I drink plenty of water, and I stay away from drama and stress. ~Reba McEntire

"Notable Quotable Anger Management Tips"

STRESS

One of the best pieces of advice I ever got was from a horse master. He told me to go slow to go fast. I think that applies to everything in life. We live as though there aren't enough hours in the day; but, if we do each thing calmly and carefully, we will get it done quicker and with much less stress. ~Viggo Mortensen

A lot of emotional stress that people go through, some people figure out a way to handle it. They have a strong enough support system to keep going and keep moving forward. And some people, they feel like they don't have that outlet. ~Terrell Owens

If you ask what is the single most important key to longevity, I would have to say it is avoiding worry, stress and tension. And if you didn't ask me, I'd still have to say it. ~George Burns

STRESS

Training gives us an outlet for suppressed energies created by stress and thus tones the spirit just as exercise conditions the body.
~Arnold Schwarzenegger

Starting a business isn't for everyone, and it's not what you should do if you aren't sure what else to do. It requires thick skin and the willingness to carry a great deal of stress, sometimes alone. It's more often a life of failure than a life of success, and the majority of successes came after a long road of disappointment and often shame. ~Kathryn Minshew

If love does not know how to give and take without restrictions, it is not love but a transaction that never fails to lay stress on a plus and a minus.
~Emma Goldman

"Notable Quotable Anger Management Tips"

STRESS

I want someone that I can have fun with and laugh with. I love to laugh, and I'm really sarcastic, so it's important that she can take a joke. I think if you are going to be with someone for a while, you really need someone you can let loose with and let go of all the stress of the day. ~Matt Lanter

The deepest fear we have, "the fear beneath all fears," is the fear of not measuring up, the fear of judgment. It's this fear that creates the stress and depression of everyday life. ~TullianTchividjian

As far as having peace within myself, the one way I can do that is forgiving the people who have done wrong to me. It causes more stress to build up anger. Peace is more productive. ~Rodney King

"Notable Quotable Anger Management Tips"

STRESS

Remember that stress doesn't come from what's going on in your life. It comes from your thoughts about what's going on in your life. ~Andrew J. Bernstein

Sometimes when people are under stress, they hate to think; and, it's the time when they most need to think. ~William J. Clinton

Much of the stress and emptiness that haunt us can be traced back to our lack of attention to beauty. Internally, the mind becomes coarse and dull if it remains unvisited by images and thoughts that hold the radiance of beauty. ~John O'Donohue

"Notable Quotable Anger Management Tips"

STRESS

I cannot stress enough that the answer to life's questions is often in people's faces. Try putting your iPhones down once in a while and look in people's faces. People's faces will tell you amazing things. Like if they are angry or nauseous or asleep.
~Amy Poehler

Doing something that is productive is a great way to alleviate emotional stress. Get your mind to doing something that is productive. ~Ziggy Marley

Running is a great way to relieve stress and clear the mind. ~Joan Van Ark

"Notable Quotable Anger Management Tips"

STRESS

Every night, I have to read a book so that my mind will stop thinking about things that I stress about.
~Britney Spears

Stress is basically a disconnection from the earth, a forgetting of the breath. Stress is an ignorant state. It believes that everything is an emergency. Nothing is that important. Just lie down. ~Natalie Goldberg

It's not just being overweight that's dangerous. Stress is dangerous. ~Carnie Wilson

"Notable Quotable Anger Management Tips"

STRESS

One sure remedy for managing your stress is to say forget everything in this moment and go to sleep because you and I can replace a number of things, but we can't replace our minds once it's lost and gone too far; so, stay balanced and centered.
~Gregory D. Anderson, Jr.

Your stress usually stems from taking on more than you can handle sometimes, so practice saying no. Saying no isn't being rude; it's keeping you from overly committing to things that make life difficult.
~Gregory D. Anderson, Jr.

Take life easy like Sunday Morning; embrace your stresses with a positive mindset; include uplifting affirmations and songs that affirm and validate you. Keep strong faith, knowing that everything will be just fine. ~Gregory D. Anderson, Jr.

On the next few lines, describe your definition of stress.

_____

_____

_____

_____

Describe the type of circumstances in which you typically experience stress. Identify the factors that trigger your stress.

_____

_____

_____

_____

How have you addressed stressful situations in the past? What tactics will you use to address stress in the future?

_____

_____

_____

_____

What advice would you give to someone in a stressful situation? How would you help this person manage stress?

_____
_____
_____
_____

_____

"Notable Quotable Anger Management Tips"

DEPRESSION

Depression is identified as an extended period of emotional changes associated with sadness and behavioral changes. Depression often causes either a significant increase or decrease in activities or behaviors such as sleeping, eating and socializing, which affects an individual's ability to function normally, their relationships and their overall mental and physical health.

(Source: American Psychological Association)

Depression is the inability to construct a future.
~Rollo May

That's the thing about depression: A human being can survive almost anything, as long as she sees the end in sight. But depression is so insidious, and it compounds daily, that it's impossible to ever see the end. The fog is like a cage without a key.
~Elizabeth Wurtzel

"Notable Quotable Anger Management Tips"

DEPRESSION

Here is the tragedy: when you are the victim of depression, not only do you feel utterly helpless and abandoned by the world, you also know that very few people can understand, or even begin to believe, that life can be this painful. There is nothing I can think of that is quite as isolating as this. ~Giles Andreae

"Notable Quotable Anger Management Tips"

DEPRESSION

At times, I feel overwhelmed and my depression leads me into darkness. ~Dorothy Hamill

Do not brood over your past mistakes and failures as this will only fill your mind with grief, regret and depression. Do not repeat them in the future. ~Swami Sivananda

It's often difficult for those who are lucky enough to have never experienced what true depression is to imagine a life of complete hopelessness, emptiness and fear. ~Susan Polis Schutz

"Notable Quotable Anger Management Tips"

DEPRESSION

Some days, 24 hours is too much to stay put in, so I take the day hour by hour, moment by moment. I break the task, the challenge, the fear into small, bite-size pieces. I can handle a piece of fear, depression, anger, pain, sadness, loneliness, illness. I actually put my hands up to my face, one next to each eye, like blinders on a horse. ~Regina Brett

Your depression is connected to your insolence and refusal to praise. ~Rumi

I have rituals for cleaning out resentments, disappointments, heartbreak, and depression for work. One of the things I do is go over old stuff if I have been unable to write for a while. ~Hubert Selby, Jr.

"Notable Quotable Anger Management Tips"

DEPRESSION

Anger is energizing. The opposite of anger is depression, which is anger turned inward.
~Gloria Steinem

The panic of the depression loosened my inhibitions against being different. I could be myself.
~Emanuel Celler

Every time you feel depressed about something, try to identify a corresponding negative thought you had just prior to and during the depression. Because these thoughts have actually created your bad mood, by learning to restructure them, you can change your mood. ~David D. Burns

DEPRESSION

The other thing is that if you rely solely on medication to manage depression or anxiety, for example, you have done nothing to train the mind, so that when you come off the medication, you are just as vulnerable to a relapse as though you had never taken the medication. ~Daniel Goleman

Time spent in nature is the most cost-effective and powerful way to counteract the burnout and sort of depression that we feel when we sit in front of a computer all day. ~Richard Louv

Recovering from the suicide of a loved one, you need all the help you can get, so I very much recommend a meditation program. The whole picture of how to recover from this has to do with body, mind, and spirit. That's applicable to any kind of depression. ~Judy Collins

"Notable Quotable Anger Management Tips"

DEPRESSION

Depression can seem worse than terminal cancer because most cancer patients feel loved and they have hope and self-esteem. ~David D. Burns

Each person's drive to overwork is unique, and doing too much numbs every workaholic's emotions differently. Sometimes overwork numbs depression, sometimes anger, sometimes envy, sometimes sexuality. Or the over-worker runs herself ragged in a race for attention. ~Arlie Russell Hochschild

Good humor is a tonic for mind and body. It is the best antidote for anxiety and depression. It is a business asset. It attracts and keeps friends. It lightens human burdens. It is the direct route to serenity and contentment. ~Grenville Kleiser

DEPRESSION

If you look at suicides, most of them are connected to depression. And the mental health system just fails them. It's so sad. We know what to do. We just don't do it. ~Rosalynn Carter

It's a recession when your neighbor loses his job; it's a depression when you lose yours. ~Harry S. Truman

Depression begins with disappointment. When disappointment festers in our soul, it leads to discouragement. ~Joyce Meyer

"Notable Quotable Anger Management Tips"

DEPRESSION

Getting better from depression demands a lifelong commitment. I've made that commitment for my life's sake and for the sake of those who love me. ~Susan Polis Schutz

Depression isn't about, "Woe is me, my life is this, that and the other'"; it's like having the worst flu all day that you just can't kick. ~Robbie Williams

What you believe is very powerful. If you have toxic emotions of fear, guilt and depression, it is because you have wrong thinking, and you have wrong thinking because of wrong believing. ~Joseph Prince

"Notable Quotable Anger Management Tips"

DEPRESSION

Get away from the place that makes you feel comfortable with your depression. The reality is it's never as bad as the insanity you've created in your head. ~Ben Huh

The five stages—denial, anger, bargaining, depression, and acceptance—are a part of the framework that makes up our learning to live with the one we lost. They are tools to help us frame and identify what we may be feeling. But they are not stops on some linear timeline in grief.
~Elisabeth Kubler-Ross

My own life was filled with so much love and joy that when depression struck, it was like a prison door slamming shut and I was being placed in an isolation cell. No one else could possibly be feeling what I was. I hated my depression and all of its symptoms.
~Susan Polis Schutz

"Notable Quotable Anger Management Tips"

DEPRESSION

Depression is very real and has pushed some of our greatest minds to commit suicide. Medication therapy, accountability partners or sponsors whom you can genuinely call on at any time is vital combined with prayer, meditation and a belief that God will help you. Journal, participate in groups, volunteer, be around positive people and keep a record of your thoughts.
~Gregory D. Anderson, Jr.

Why are you feeling depressed? What has you in this spider web that you just can't let go of for some reason? Use these affirmations; say: I will not worry about anything, my God is in full control. I have no fear; I have peace, and all is well. Life is good. I feel so good. I am happy; I am in peace; I feel relaxed; and, I am calm. I love God and God Loves Me. I have no fear, and I am never scared. I trust God to carry me, cover me and to protect me at all times. I will worry about nothing and pray about everything. Amen (Repeat as often as necessary)
~Gregory D. Anderson, Jr.

"Notable Quotable Anger Management Tips"

DEPRESSION

Come out of your depression now knowing that there is NOTHING to worry about. We are all here for a short period of time. You have an assignment which involves not just getting all you can get and being greedy; it means a life of helping others. Go and volunteer to feed the hungry. What are you doing for others? Start helping others and get out of your own way by listening to someone else. Stop the pity party and realize that we all have problems and each one can be overcome, a little at a time. Prepare for the marathon and endure in faith and action until the end. ~Gregory D. Anderson, Jr.

On the next few lines, describe your definition of depression. What is the difference between sadness and depression?

_____

_____

_____

_____

In moments of depression, how do you typically feel? What are your thoughts during these moments?

_____

_____

_____

_____

Do you think it is possible to beat depression? What tactics are needed to do so?

_____

_____

_____

_____

Imagine you have the chance to revisit your lowest point in life. How would you handle this situation differently?

_____

_____

_____

_____

_____

"Notable Quotable Anger Management Tips"

LONELINESS

Loneliness is defined as emotional distress caused by the lack of social interaction with others. Individuals who experience loneliness believe they lack significant relationships and long for relationships with others, which triggers sadness, isolation and unfulfillment.

(Source: Psychology Today)

Pray that your loneliness may spur you into finding something to live for, great enough to die for.
~Dag Hammarskjold

Loneliness is my least favorite thing about life. The thing that I'm most worried about is just being alone without anybody to care for or someone who will care for me. ~Anne Hathaway

My peers, lately, have found companionship through means of intoxication—it makes them sociable. I, however, cannot force myself to use drugs to cheat on my loneliness—it is all that I have—and when the drugs and alcohol dissipate, it will be all that my peers have as well. ~Franz Kafk

LONELINESS

Who knows what true loneliness is—not the conventional word but the naked terror? To the lonely themselves it wears a mask. The most miserable outcast hugs some memory or some illusion.
~Joseph Conrad

I've also seen that great men are often lonely. This is understandable because they have built such high standards for themselves that they often feel alone. But that same loneliness is part of their ability to create. ~Yousuf Karsh

Everybody has something that chews them up and, for me, that thing was always loneliness. The cinema has the power to make you not feel lonely, even when you are. ~Tom Hanks

"Notable Quotable Anger Management Tips"

LONELINESS

Loneliness comes with life. ~Whitney Houston

Loneliness is never more cruel than when it is felt in close propinquity with someone who has ceased to communicate. ~Germaine Greer

To be poor does not mean you lack the means to extend charity to another. You may lack money or food, but you have the gift of friendship to overwhelm the loneliness that grips the lives of so many. ~Stanley Hauerwas

"Notable Quotable Anger Management Tips"

LONELINESS

Music was my refuge. I could crawl into the space between the notes and curl my back to loneliness. ~Maya Angelou

Loneliness is the poverty of self; solitude is the richness of self. ~May Sarton

Everything we do is for the purpose of altering consciousness. We form friendships so that we can feel certain emotions, like love, and avoid others, like loneliness. We eat specific foods to enjoy their fleeting presence on our tongues. We read for the pleasure of thinking another person's thoughts. ~Sam Harris

"Notable Quotable Anger Management Tips"

LONELINESS

What should young people do with their lives today? Many things, obviously. But the most daring thing is to create stable communities in which the terrible disease of loneliness can be cured. ~Kurt Vonnegut

We live in a society bloated with data yet starved for wisdom. We're connected 24/7, yet anxiety, fear, depression and loneliness are at an all-time high. We must course-correct.
~Elizabeth Kapu'uwailani Lindsey

Love is something far more than desire for sexual intercourse; it is the principal means of escape from the loneliness which afflicts most men and women throughout the greater part of their lives.
~Bertrand Russell

LONELINESS

But I also think all of the great stories in literature deal with loneliness. Sometimes it's by way of heartbreak, sometimes it's by way of injustice, sometimes it's by way of fate. There's an infinite number of ways to examine it. ~Tom Hanks

Look for yourself, and you will find in the long run only hatred, loneliness, despair, rage, ruin, and decay. But look for Christ, and you will find Him, and with Him everything else thrown in. ~C. S. Lewis

Why do I write? It's not that I want people to think I am smart, or even that I am a good writer. I write because I want to end my loneliness. ~Jonathan Safran Foer

"Notable Quotable Anger Management Tips"

LONELINESS

But the battles against loneliness that I fought when I was 16 are very different from those I fought when I was 27, and those are very different from the ones I fight at 44. ~Tom Hanks

Suffering, failure, loneliness, sorrow, discouragement, and death will be part of your journey, but the Kingdom of God will conquer all these horrors. No evil can resist grace forever. ~Brennan Manning

Because of my childhood where I was constantly by myself, I always feel lonely. I have a lot of people that I absolutely love and I know love me, but I can't get rid of that feeling of loneliness no matter who I'm with - even with my children. ~Natalia Vodianova

"Notable Quotable Anger Management Tips"

LONELINESS

We have all known the long loneliness, and we have found that the answer is community. ~Dorothy Day

Yoga is a way to freedom. By its constant practice, we can free ourselves from fear, anguish and loneliness. ~Indra Devi

Everyone desires relationships and community. Most people want to belong to a cohesive, like-minded group. It starves off loneliness. It promotes identity. These are natural and very human instincts. ~Joshua Ferris

"Notable Quotable Anger Management Tips"

LONELINESS

I said it's a cold universe, and I don't mean that metaphorically. If you go out into space, it's cold. It's really cold, and we don't know what's up there. We happen to be in this little pocket where there's a sun. What have we got except love and each other to guard against all that isolation and loneliness? ~David Chase

I have a lot of friends, but my biggest fear is loneliness. I miss my family in Mumbai, and my biggest nightmare every day is to go back home alone. ~Deepika Padukone

One of the things reading does, it makes your loneliness manageable if you are an essentially lonely person. ~Jamaica Kincaid

"Notable Quotable Anger Management Tips"

LONELINESS

The end of the road for most of us is when we isolate ourselves from others and fail to talk to ourselves in positive affirmation. Also, when we start to avoid people is the beginning of loneliness.
~Gregory D. Anderson, Jr.

Write and keep a journal. Chart all your travels and day to day activities; this will allow you to look back over your life to see how you traveled and lived. Play games, smell the trees, travel, have conversations with others and make new friends. Live wisely and don't allow loneliness to dominate your world in any shape form or fashion. Read, eat great foods, take walks, join groups and stay active as best you can.
~Gregory D. Anderson, Jr.

"Notable Quotable Anger Management Tips"

LONELINESS

Communicate, keep in touch, keep a journal, watch great movies, speak up and read God's great word. Maybe it's time to tell your story: write your book, write that film or go mentor some young man or woman. Check on them and teach them some things you know that may help them now or down the road. Find an organization you would like to volunteer for and be a strong part of it by letting your voice be heard. ~Gregory D. Anderson Jr

On the next few lines, describe your definition of loneliness.

_____

_____

_____

_____

What is the difference between being alone and feeling lonely?

_____

_____

_____

_____

How do you typically cope with loneliness? Describe your thoughts, behaviors and emotions during periods of loneliness.

_____

_____

_____

_____

_____

Imagine you have been placed on a deserted island with only basic necessities for survival. What tactics would you use to cope with loneliness during this time?

_____

_____

_____

_____

_____

LOSS

Loss is identified as a traumatic event that alters the course of an individual's life. Loss can be caused by a death, separation or divorce, injury, illness or other major life events that affect an individual's emotional stability, identity, relationships and beliefs. During a period of loss, individuals often question their lives and their circumstances.

(Source: Psychology Today)

Death is not the greatest loss in life. The greatest loss is what dies inside us while we live. ~Norman Cousins

There is no better than adversity. Every defeat, every heartbreak, every loss contains its own seed, its own lesson on how to improve your performance the next time. ~Malcolm X

In life, loss is inevitable. Everyone knows this, yet in the core of most people it remains deeply denied—"This should not happen to me." It is for this reason that loss is the most difficult challenge one has to face as a human being. ~Dayananda Saraswati

"Notable Quotable Anger Management Tips"

LOSS

Fear seems to have many causes. Fear of loss, fear of failure, fear of being hurt, and so on, but ultimately all fear is the ego's fear of death, of annihilation. To the ego, death is always just around the corner. In this mind-identified state, fear of death affects every aspect of your life. ~Eckhart Toll

Getting over someone is a grieving process. You mourn the loss of the relationship, and that's only expedited by "Out of sight, out of mind." But when you walk outside and see them on a billboard or on TV or on the cover of a magazine, it reopens the wound. It's a high-class problem, but it's real. ~Hank Azaria

A great man is one who leaves others at a loss after he is gone. ~Paul Valery

LOSS

Loss doesn't feel redeemable. But for me one consoling aspect is the recognition that, in this at least, none of us is different from anyone else: We all lose loved ones; we all face our own death.
~Meghan O'Rourke

When you lose something in your life, stop thinking it's a loss for you . . . it is a gift you have been given so you can get on the right path to where you are meant to go, not to where you think you should have gone.
~Suze Orman

I am concerned about ageism and the loss of beauty—the perception that as you grow older, you "lose your looks," which I think is diabolical.
~Erin O'Connor

"Notable Quotable Anger Management Tips"

LOSS

Sometimes a loss is the best thing that can happen. It teaches you what you should have done next time. ~Snoop Dogg

We never understand how little we need in this world until we know the loss of it. ~James M. Barrie

Loss is nothing else but change, and change is Nature's delight. ~Marcus Aurelius

"Notable Quotable Anger Management Tips"

LOSS

Grief is in two parts. The first is loss. The second is the remaking of life. ~Anne Roiphe

Success consists of going from failure to failure without loss of enthusiasm. ~Winston Churchill

Bad things do happen; how I respond to them defines my character and the quality of my life. I can choose to sit in perpetual sadness, immobilized by the gravity of my loss, or I can choose to rise from the pain and treasure the most precious gift I have—life itself. ~Walter Anderson

"Notable Quotable Anger Management Tips"

LOSS

A family is a risky venture because the greater the love, the greater the loss . . . That's the trade-off. But I'll take it all. ~Brad Pitt

For what shall it profit a man, if he gain the whole world and suffer the loss of his soul? ~Jesus Christ

The acknowledgment of our weakness is the first step in repairing our loss. ~Thomas a Kempis

"Notable Quotable Anger Management Tips"

LOSS

And yet, I suppose you mourn the loss or the death of what you thought your life was, even if you find your life is better after. You mourn the future that you thought you'd planned. ~Lynn Redgrave

When I spoke, I was listened to; and I was at a loss to know how I had so easily acquired the art of commanding attention, and giving the tone to the conversation. ~Adelbert von Chamisso

The best way to guarantee a loss is to quit.
~Morgan Freeman

"Notable Quotable Anger Management Tips"

LOSS

Where do we enroll in Life 101? Where are the classes dealing with the loss of a job, the death of a loved one, the failure of a relationship? Unfortunately, those lessons are mostly learned through trial by fire and the school of hard knocks. ~Les Brown

The loss of a friend is like that of a limb; time may heal the anguish of the wound, but the loss cannot be repaired. ~Robert Southey

Waste is worse than loss. The time is coming when every person who lays claim to ability will keep the question of waste before him constantly. The scope of thrift is limitless. ~Thomas A. Edison

"Notable Quotable Anger Management Tips"

LOSS

Loss and possession, death and life are one. There falls no shadow where there shines no sun.
~Hilaire Belloc

The Lord compensates the faithful for every loss. That which is taken away from those who love the Lord will be added unto them in his own way. While it may not come at the time we desire, the faithful will know that every tear today will eventually be returned a hundredfold with tears of rejoicing and gratitude.
~Joseph B. Wirthlin

Prefer a loss to a dishonest gain; the one brings pain at the moment, the other for all time. ~Chilon

"Notable Quotable Anger Management Tips"

LOSS

Loss unfortunately is a part of this thing we call life. None of us will escape this walk or race alive; however it is my perspective that I have gathered over time is to smile, buckle up and enjoy the ride, but it does stop sooner or later. ~Gregory D. Anderson, Jr.

Losing a loved one hurts; I recall losing my grandfather and wasn't in position to attend his funeral. I also recall two other times when losing a loved one hurt. I was about to attend the funeral of my uncle Pretty Boy Floyd whom we called Lil Brother; he was younger than me and like a brother or a cousin. When I heard about his passing, I was very hurt and it immediately made me think about my own personal mortality. I wept greatly. The other time when loss hurt was when I heard about my high school friend Joseph Cotton whom we shared many memories. I couldn't make it to his funeral either, but I loved him like a brother. I drove up to the steps of the church sat in my car and cried. Loss is very hurtful, but we somehow, in time, find a way to treasure our loved ones in our memories. Through the good, bad and ugly, we survive! ~Gregory D. Anderson, Jr.

"Notable Quotable Anger Management Tips"

LOSS

I see loss as God's way of being UNSELFISH towards man because if we all just remained here on earth then none of us would survive because there would be FAMINE eventually and lack of food and water. We are here to enjoy our time, create great memories and to love one another. ~Gregory D. Anderson, Jr.

On the next few lines, describe your definition of loss.

_____

_____

_____

_____

What has been your greatest loss? How did you cope with this loss?

_____

_____

_____

_____

_____

What do you now believe is the best way to handle loss and grief? Have you applied this strategy to your own life?

_____

_____

_____

_____

_____

If you could restore anything you have lost for a day, what would it be? How would you spend this day?

_____

_____

_____

_____

_____

"Notable Quotable Anger Management Tips"

EMOTIONAL INTELLIGENCE

EQ

Emotional intelligence (EQ) defines an individual's ability to understand and manage their emotions as well as the emotions of other individuals. Emotional intelligence involves three skills: the ability to recognize emotions, the ability to apply emotions and the ability to manage emotions. Individuals who experience difficulties with emotional intelligence may find it difficult to cope with their own emotions and to understand the emotions of others.

(Source: Psychology Today)

Empathy and social skills are social intelligence, the interpersonal part of emotional intelligence. That's why they are alike. ~Daniel Goleman

Emotional intelligence is your ability to recognize and understand emotions in yourself and others and your ability to use this awareness to manage your behavior and relationships. ~Travis Bradberry

"Notable Quotable Anger Management Tips"

EMOTIONAL INTELLIGENCE

EQ

Exceptional employees don't possess God-given personality traits; they rely on simple, everyday EQ skills that anyone can incorporate into their repertoire.
~Travis Bradberry

"Notable Quotable Anger Management Tips"

EMOTIONAL INTELLIGENCE

EQ

Emotional intelligence begins to develop in the earliest years. All the small exchanges children have with their parents, teachers, and with each other carry emotional messages. ~Daniel Goleman

Emotional intelligence is the ability to identify and manage your own emotions and the emotions of others. ~Psychology Today

Some of the greatest moments in human history were fueled by emotional intelligence. ~The Atlantic

"Notable Quotable Anger Management Tips"

EMOTIONAL INTELLIGENCE

EQ

The ability to manage your emotions and remain calm under pressure has a direct link to your performance. ~Forbes

We have found that 90% of top performers are skilled at managing their emotions in times of stress in order to remain calm and in control. ~TalentSmart

We probably all know people, either at work or in our personal lives, who are really good listeners. No matter what kind of situation we're in, they always seem to know just what to say—and how to say it—so that we're not offended or upset. They're caring and considerate, and even if we don't find a solution to our problem, we usually leave feeling more hopeful and optimistic. ~MindTools

"Notable Quotable Anger Management Tips"

EMOTIONAL INTELLIGENCE

EQ

Emotional Intelligence is Self Awareness, Self Regulation, Motivation, Empathy and Social Skills.
~Alyson

Emotional intelligence is the ability to identify and monitor emotions—your own and others'.
~Daniel Goleman

If you don't control your emotions, your emotions will control your acts, and that's not good.
~Mariano Rivera

"Notable Quotable Anger Management Tips"

EMOTIONAL INTELLIGENCE

EQ

When we direct our thoughts properly, we can control our emotions. ~W. Clement Stone

When I passed the age of 50, I learned how to control my emotions. ~Mahmoud Darwish

Take control of your consistent emotions and begin to consciously and deliberately reshape your daily experience of life. ~Tony Robbins

"Notable Quotable Anger Management Tips"

EMOTIONAL INTELLIGENCE

EQ

One of the reasons I was so unhappy for years was because I never embraced my emotions and I was trying to stay in control. ~Demi Lovato

Negative emotions will challenge your grit every step of the way. While it's impossible not to feel your emotions, it's completely under your power to manage them effectively and to keep yourself in a position of control. When you let your emotions overtake your ability to think clearly, it's easy to lose your resolve. ~Travis Bradberry

The brain is a complex biological organ possessing immense computational capability: it constructs our sensory experience, regulates our thoughts and emotions, and controls our actions. ~Eric Kandel

"Notable Quotable Anger Management Tips"

EMOTIONAL INTELLIGENCE

EQ

Our lives are pretty calm. Merging on the freeway is the closest you get to risking your life. So what's missing now is that primal emotion of being scared to death, and I think that's why people crave thrills like roller coasters or scary movies. They give you the chance to feel this very primal emotion in a very controlled environment. ~Oren Peli

Being irrational and out of control is what happens in real life. Not cautiously choreographing your anger or your emotions, losing yourself in them is what happens in real life. ~Margot Robbie

"Notable Quotable Anger Management Tips"

EMOTIONAL INTELLIGENCE

EQ

Beautiful sights arouse feelings of love, and contrary sights bring feelings of disgrace and hate. And the emotions of the soul and spirit bring something additional to the body itself, which exists under the control of the soul and the direction of the spirit. ~Giordano Bruno

I'm much softer than people think. I don't present to the world an emotional face. I'm pretty good at self-control, but I am easily moved. ~Christopher Le

New York Times science writer Goleman argues that our emotions play a much greater role in thought, decision making and individual success than is commonly acknowledged. ~New York Times

"Notable Quotable Anger Management Tips"

EMOTIONAL INTELLIGENCE

EQ

If your emotional abilities aren't in hand, if you don't have self-awareness, if you are not able to manage your distressing emotions, if you can't have empathy and have effective relationships, then no matter how smart you are, you are not going to get very far.
~Daniel Goleman

When our emotional health is in a bad state, so is our level of self-esteem. We have to slow down and deal with what is troubling us, so that we can enjoy the simple joy of being happy and at peace with ourselves. ~Jess Scott

The only way to change someone's mind is to connect with them from the heart. ~Rasheed Ogunlaru

"Notable Quotable Anger Management Tips"

EMOTIONAL INTELLIGENCE

EQ

Teachers need to be comfortable talking about feelings. This is part of teaching emotional literacy—a set of skills we can all develop, including the ability to read, understand, and respond appropriately to one's own emotions and the emotions of others.
~Daniel Goleman

Life is a juggling act with your own emotions. The trick is to always keep something in your hand and something in the air. ~Chloe Thurlow

Our feelings are not there to be cast out or conquered. They're there to be engaged and expressed with imagination and intelligence. ~T. K. Coleman

"Notable Quotable Anger Management Tips"

EMOTIONAL INTELLIGENCE

EQ

Never let your emotions overtake you in the heat of the moment; take your time to think out a few things you can do to better address or resolve a matter.
~Gregory D. Anderson, Jr.

Emotional Intelligence is always needed in leadership in order to better navigate unruly employees, staff or coworkers. Emotional intelligence listens and shows concern. ~Gregory D. Anderson, Jr.

If you let your emotions overthrow you during an argument or a disagreement or at a time that you feel that you are at your most vulnerable state, chances are that you won't be using Emotional Intelligence.
~Gregory D. Anderson, Jr.

On the next few lines, describe your definition of emotional intelligence.

_____

_____

_____

_____

How has emotional intelligence made you more aware of your own emotions? How has it made you more aware of others' emotions?

_____

_____

_____

_____

_____

Do you believe you are born with emotional intelligence, or is it something you acquire through experience?

_____

_____

_____

_____

How is emotional intelligence related to the previously discussed topics (Anger, Stress, Depression, Loneliness and Loss)?

_____

_____

_____

_____

_____

In conclusion, we all wrestle with different thoughts that can drive us to the point of no return, but it is important for us to learn how to control our anger and not to be controlled by our anger. My desire is that these quotes will be nuggets of wisdom that will move you to monitor both your personal and professional progress. Begin your progress today!

It is my hope that you will benefit greatly from this book. In reading at least a quote or two per day and answering the questions at the end of each chapter, you are becoming closer not only to managing your anger but also to understanding your anger. Journal your thoughts and feelings in order to gain insight into the inner workings of your emotions and to better manage your anger, stress, depression, loneliness, loss and your emotional intelligence. Become more aware of the issue to discover the best solution.

If you need an anger management assessment or an anger management class for you or your loved ones, please call Texas Anger Managers at 832-329-7148 or visit www.TexasAngerManagers.com.

Thank you for your purchase and may this resource deeply enrich you and bless your mind, body and spirit.

REFERENCES

"Anger." American Psychological Association. American Psychological Association, n.d. Web. 28 Mar. 2016.

"Depression." American Psychological Association. American Psychological Association, n.d. Web. 28 Mar. 2016.

"Emotional Intelligence." Psychology Today. Psychology Today, n.d. Web. 28 Mar. 2016.

Marano, Hara Estroff. "The Dangers of Loneliness." Psychology Today. Psychology Today, 1 July 2003. Web. 28 Mar. 2016.

"Understanding Chronic Stress." American Psychological Association. American Psychological Association, n.d. Web. 28 Mar. 2016.

Winch, Guy, Ph.D. "The 5 Psychological Challenges of Loss and Grief." Psychology Today. Psychology Today, 1 Apr. 2014. Web. 28 Mar. 2016.

Made in the USA
Monee, IL
19 June 2022